Household Tools and Tasks

By ELMER L. SMITH

Photography by J. MORGAN SINCOCK

APPLIED ARTS PUBLISHERS

Third Printing 1987 GCIU Lebanon, Pennsylvania 17042

ISBN 0-911410-47-3

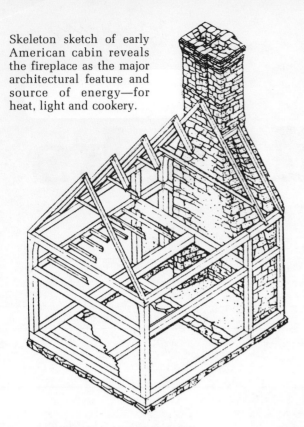

Skeleton sketch of early American cabin reveals the fireplace as the major architectural feature and source of energy—for heat, light and cookery.

Cast iron fireplace fender.

Fireplace Necessities

It has been estimated that as late as 1800 wood supplied ninety-four percent of all our energy other than wind and sunlight or human muscle that was used in America. Wood for the household had to be snaked from the forest, cut into fireplace or stove length, split when necessary and kept under cover. To heat a cabin in winter in northern regions it required approximately twenty cords of wood—which is a woodpile between 120 and 150 feet in length! that's a lot of chopping and hauling.

Perhaps the first domestic problem of early settlers was that of providing heat for their dwellings and for their cooking. The fireplace was the only source of heat in the early cabins and, as a result, many early artifacts are directly related to the hearth, commonly the center of family activity.

Although architectural styles varied regionally from New England to the Southern colonies most early houses had one basic similarity—they were usually one room, loft, and fireplace, the fireplace being the major functioning unit. Since the discovery of fire, man has attempted to perfect methods of harnessing its vast potential. But little permanent improvement beyond the fireplace and masonry chimney emerged in the field of heating until the eighteenth century brought the concept of convection for heat distribution.

Fireplace objects were among the limited possessions not home-made. Often prized, as evidenced by early wills, which listed "a skillet or kittle" and to whom they were to be handed down after death!

Fireplace artifacts included cranes, trammels, skewers, toasters, waffle irons, grills, trivets, tongs, log hooks, toasting forks and a variety of cooking utensils such as iron pots, kettles and pans. The crane usually hung against the back wall of the fireplace and could swing back and forth over the hearth. From this pot hooks were suspended on which cauldrons or kettles were swung over the fire.

Andirons (originally called hand-irons or fire dogs) were used to raise wood from the flat hearth so as to increase the draft and produce a higher heat. Of various sizes and shapes, some provided attachments to facilitate cookery, or fenders to prevent embers from flying beyond the stone hearth.

In 1742 Benjamin Franklin invented an open stove

At lower left are two foot warmers used with live coals. They were portable for use wherever desired. The tin brown-bread pan makes two 10″ loaves, placed near the burning embers of the open hearth.

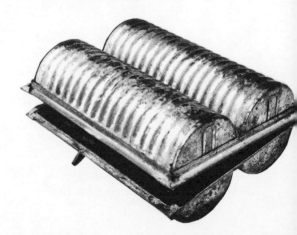

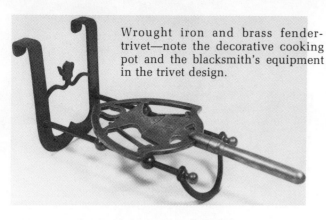

Wrought iron and brass fender-trivet—note the decorative cooking pot and the blacksmith's equipment in the trivet design.

consisting of cast iron plates—a major development that was soon in much demand. American ironmasters produced a wide variety of iron stoves and the fireplace declined in importance as the source of heat, light and warmth.

Fireplace artifacts were generally of forged or cast iron. Such objects included three-legged forged trivets with long handles for hanging near the fireplace when not in use; skewers; forks for toasting or roasting; chains with hooks so that cooking utensils could be hung over live coals; trammels with adjustable positioning for hanging objects at varying heights over the fire.

Illustrated are a matching pair of utensils for poking and rearranging logs and a forged shovel to remove ashes and live coals. Tongs could be used to pick up live coals to place in foot warmers; bed warmers; smoothing irons and similar household equipment.

The iron wafer and waffle irons with two heavy patterned plates were attached by rivets to scissor-like handles.

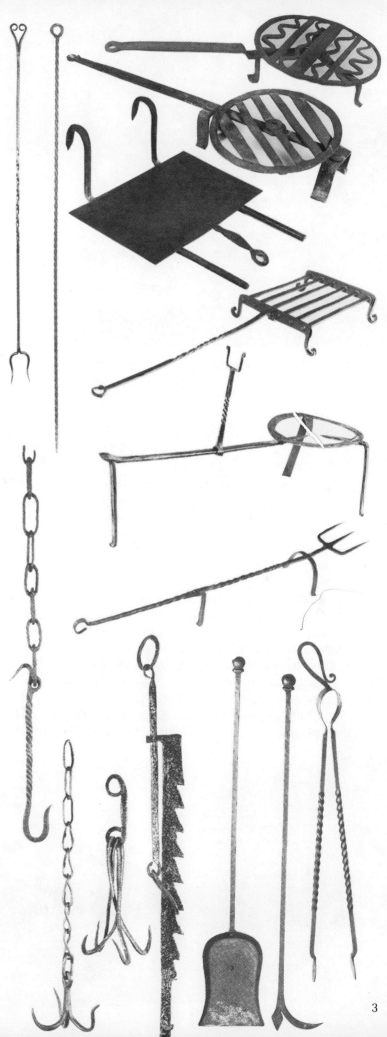

3

Walking wheel at Sublets Tavern, Powhatan, Virginia, and spinning jenny *(below right)* from the Mary Washington House, Fredericksburg, Virginia.

Flax hackle with both coarse and fine tooth comb; wire and wood combs and a hand-made wooden flax comb.

Spinning and Weaving

SHEEP were raised on many farms. The womenfolk processed the wool by cleaning, carding and spinning it into yarn. Carding wool was done with hand-cards and the resulting rolls of wood fibre were spun on hand-wheels. A days work yielded from five to six skeins. Some wove the yarn into cloth on the loom from which the family clothing was cut and sewn.

Linen was also needed for sheets, bedding and clothing, the flax being raised in the farm fields. Sown in May, housewives harvested in late summer by pulling the plants from the roots and spreading them on the ground. After several days they were tied into bundles, stacked and immersed in water. Next they were denuded of debris and leaves and set upright to dry in the sun.

Flax was then ready for the brake—an ancient heavy wooden tool that by constant lifting and dropping dealt heavy blows on the flax which separated the woody pulp from the fibre. Fibres were then placed in bundles to be swingled and scraped with a wooden

4

blade and then beaten with a wooden pestle-mallet device until softened.

Finally the fibres were drawn through a heckle which cleaned and straightened them—the first time through the wide-toothed comb-like device and the second time through a finer heckle. Then it was ready to be spun into thread or linen yarn.

Obviously the preparation of the field-grown flax was a long and arduous process. Actual spinning could be done on cold nights near the fireplace or at odd hours.

After the flax was spun it was reeled from the spools and made into skeins which were soaked in warm water and later bucked in lye water made from leached wood ashes, then rinsed, beaten, washed and dried and wound into balls ready for weaving.

The natural color would be a musty yellow and the only commercial product available for dyeing was indigo—otherwise plants were used to create various shades and tints. These had to be fixed with a mordant so the color would hold—so the dyed yarn was soaked in ash-hopper lye or urine.

One common wool color was gray, which could be obtained by spinning together white wool, black wool and wool dyed in indigo—about one-third each.

A loom dominated the room, being a frame of four square timber posts about the size of a full-sized poster bed; so it was often placed in a shed, loft or special weaving room.

Custom weavers sometimes converted thread and yarn into cloth.

The loom was a device from early antiquity, and weaving, along with the work of the potter, was one of the traditional ancient crafts.

Early loom at Ash Lawn (Highlands home of President James Monroe) Charlottesville Virginia. Assorted loom and weaving artifacts and a ribbon loom. *(Lower right)*.

Alphabet Sampler (1852) by Martha E. Haines, Maryland. Young children learned their letters while also being taught sewing and embroidering.

Hand made yarn reels (*upper left*) Vermont and (*lower right*) Maine—note the hand-carved wooden gears that actually count the skeins.

Needlecraft frame, Mary Washington House, Fredericksburg, Virginia.

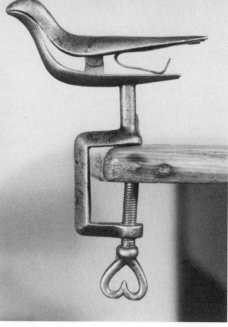

Genealogical sampler by Margaret B. Webster, Berks County, Pennsylvania (circa 1830).

Sewing birds were a decorative but useful clamp, common in the 1800's, to hold fabric while it was being stitched. The beak served as a clamp and the tail served as the lever!

The Machine that Invaded the Home

PERHAPS the most important domestic labor-saving device in the 19th century was the sewing machine. By far much more complicated and precise than any other household machine of the time, it was the first mechanically accurate piece of equipment that enjoyed wide use in the homes of America.

The first machine with promise for success was invented by J. J. Greenough in 1842, followed by a model of Elias Howe in 1845. The first Singer machine in 1851 contained 150 standardized and separately made parts—a major breakthrough in technology involving division of labor and specialization, in contrast with traditional hand-made machines of an earlier period.

New Royal 1887 patented model by Illinois Sewing Machine Company, Chicago. This console type machine avoided the earlier iron-machine look which was not an attractive household addition. The top flips back to lift up the machine, and it doubles as a working table. Drawers contain spools and sewing equipment. Housing such mechanisms became a problem as manufacturers strove to relate to the furnishings of parlor or living room. (The console became a trend as radio and television.)

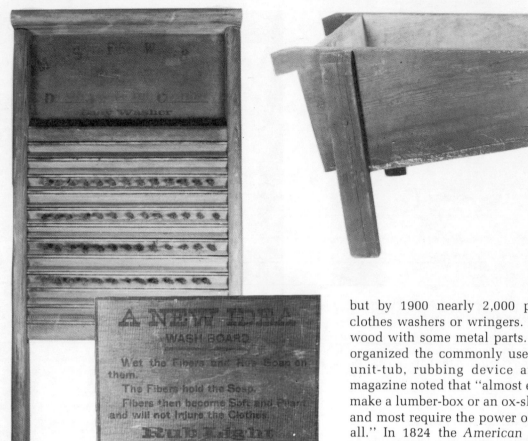

Mechanical Washing

Care of the family clothing and household white wear was a constant chore—Monday being the traditional day for such activities, which was in addition to the regular daily tasks.

Most washing was done in a wooden tub with a wash board. Clothing was boiled in a kettle over a wood fire, scrubbed with home-made soap, rinsed and hung up to dry on outdoor lines.

The first washing machine was patented in 1805 but by 1900 nearly 2,000 patents were filed on clothes washers or wringers. Early washers were of wood with some metal parts. Basically they merely organized the commonly used equipment into one unit-tub, rubbing device and board. One rural magazine noted that "almost every bungler who can make a lumber-box or an ox-sled has invented them, and most require the power of the ox to use them at all." In 1824 the *American Agricultural Encyclopedia* criticized the existing machines stating "American Yankee ingenuity would seem to have exhausted itself in the making of washing machines..." yet it noted, "no one has continued in so much favor as *Doty's Paragon* which came on the market in 1820." The Universal clothes wringer with wooden rollers was also well accepted during that period.

Two mechanical washers are shown. The *Ross Perfection* uses the rocking, rubbing, squeezing technique. Other early washing machines used the churning and/or dash-wheel method similar to a butter churn.

The *Typhoon Washer*, featuring patented ball-bearings, was made by the Richmond Cedar Works, Virginia, and has a wringer device and moveable

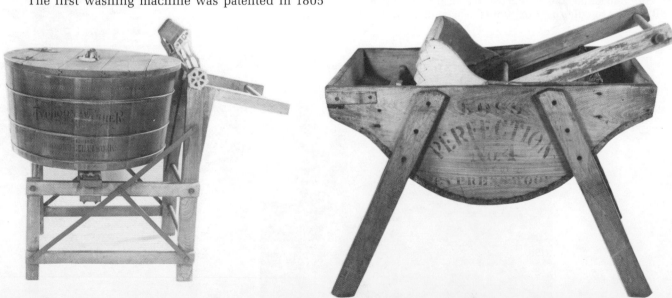

stand for a rinsing tub. This model is very similar in design to later electrified types which combined rocking and dasher action.

In addition to the laborious task of washing, the clothes had to be ironed with heavy cast weights, or sheets may be simply smoothed with a wooden board. Early ironing boards for sleeves and Mrs. Days' waist and sleeve board *(lower left)*, patented in 1891.

Soap Before Procter & Gamble

IN EARLY TIMES butchering had its by-products— mutton or sheep fat went into tallow for making dipped taper candles, and hog fat was made into lard. Beef fat and refuse fat—good for nothing else—went into soap.

Grease was collected in containers, and ashes from the wood-fired stove in kitchen and fireplace were kept to leach into lye. Soap-making was a seasonal task, often in both fall and spring. Ashes kept for the purpose were placed in the hopper. (See illustration upper facing page.) This wooden tub was slanted with a drain at the bottom. Straw was placed in the tub, then ashes were dumped in and water was sprinkled over the filled tub. When the water seeped through the ashes and drained out of the spout, it was lye water. (Boiled down this made a crude potash or pearlash.)

In the meantime the grease was boiled in a large outdoor kettle, constantly skimmed with a brass skimmer or paddle to remove any undissolved particles. When the lye water and grease were boiled and stirred together the result was soap. Easiest to make was the soft liquid soap which was stored in a barrel. Hard soap took more lye and longer boiling. Of a yellowish color, while still soft it was cut into bars and stored in brown paper in the wash house.

Scouring: Prior to 1900 every family had large quantities of tinware, which often collected a coating of carbon and baked-on overflow of ingredients difficult to remove. In some regions a scouring day followed soap making, when all the tinware was boiled in the liquid soap-making residue, then cleaned and polished with fine white sand or powdered whiting.

Stoneware mug and red earthenware custard cup.

Pottery of Utility

ON these pages are displayed a sampling of the wide variety of pottery products.

Earthenware making was widespread throughout America. Every community of significance had a pottery where utilitarian containers were produced. While early pottery was often crude, unglazed and undecorated, by 1750 some potters created attractive stoneware, glazed and decorated pieces.

The vast proportion of the products fulfilled a domestic demand for storing cider, distilled spirits, apple butter, butter, milk and other foodstuffs for the family larder.

Much of the tableware of early America consisted of pottery plus wooden trenchers or iron. So potters made a wide variety of objects such as bowls, jars, mugs, platters, wash bowls, pitchers, pie plates, cullenders and table plates. But such utensils and cooking ware were heavy, inconvenient and not very durable, so they were replaced by tinware and other materials that became available by the end of the nineteen century.

Crocks, jugs and flower pots were made in an unbelievable variety of sizes and shapes—no standardization then!

The stoneware mug and red earthenware custard cup (above) were for individual use. The two ink-wells (below) were necessities before the days of fountain and ballpoint pens. Home-made beverages

Two ink wells and stoneware bottles, one marked root beer. Such containers were used for home-made beverages common in the summer months.

such as ginger ale and root beer, common in the summer months, call for "returnable" bottles.

Dough for pancakes and similar delights was prepared and poured from brown-glazed batter jugs such as the specimen at top left of Page 11.

Clay smoking pipe bowls were common (with home-made wooden stems). These were used as much by females as males, many country women smoked in their leisure hours—that is, until the practice was replaced with dipping snuff!

At right are other objects of interest—a sugar bowl with unglazed exterior and heavily glazed interior and next to it a snuff jar and Turk's Head cake mold in redware. The large bowl next to the pipes is from the Bennington Pottery.

In 1865 such pieces were reasonably priced and Rockingham Stoneware sold at $3.50 per dozen for one gallon jugs and 6 quart pitchers were less than a dollar each. But by the turn of the century potters found little demand for their products.

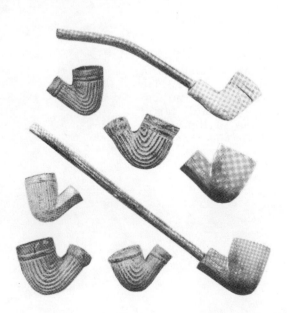

Lighting Equipment

Striking a fire was a painstaking task before matches emerged in 1827. Little Wonder that friction matches were considered one of man's most ingenious and important inventions. Flint struck against iron or steel created a spark which *might* fall into the tinder box and ignite—it could take an half hour or more to start a simple flame—in damp weather it was nearly impossible!

The early pioneer settlers had sunlight and firelight, so to bed at dark and up at dawn. Later pine knot torches were used, then rushes soaked in grease and finally the grease betty-lamp. Oil and other liquid fuels came still later.

Animal fats were transformed into crude candles giving off a horrible smoke and smell. Better quality candles came from bees-wax or boiled bayberries processed at home.

Tallow dips were the early type candles, made from the fatty part of sheep and beef. Heated over the stove until most of the tallow melted away, the rest

Two-piece tin match box and holder patented in 1873 offers a place to strike the huge wooden matches. Reliable "lucifer matches" were thought to be poisonous, so the box covers refutes this folklore.

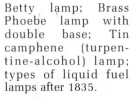

Betty lamp; Brass Phoebe lamp with double base; Tin camphene (turpentine-alcohol) lamp; types of liquid fuel lamps after 1835.

Candle boxes that stand or hang on the wall.

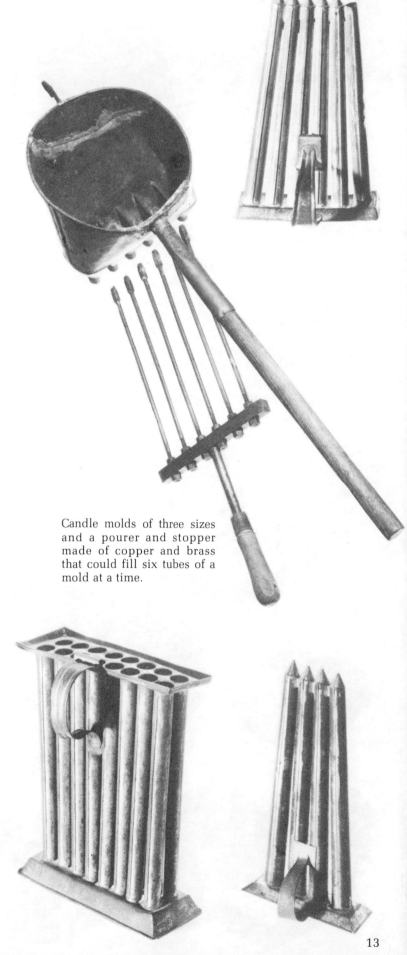

was pressed in a cloth sack in a lard squeezer until all but the tissue was removed.

Wicks were from tow, looped over sticks. This tow was dipped in a kettle of melted tallow and removed briefly to allow it to cool, redipped continually until the dips became thicker and thicker, and finally hung up to season.

When the tinsmiths made molds available, these were eagerly sought after as labor-saving devices. In molds the wick was inserted and hot tallow was poured into the tubes—a simple one-step operation, with some molds making as many as three dozen at a pouring. To remove them the mold was placed in hot water and the candles slipped out easily to be stored in candle boxes or tins.

Candle molds of three sizes and a pourer and stopper made of copper and brass that could fill six tubes of a mold at a time.

Earthenware to Tin

TINWARE, made available throughout America by New England itinerant peddlers, was in great demand. Widely adopted as the basic material for plates, dishpans, mugs, pots, dippers, graters, pails, pie plates, funnels, percolators and numerous other objects, it was a great improvement over pottery.

Two Irish immigrants who set up shop in Connecticut in 1738 created the first American made tinware. But it wasn't until after the Revolution that the ware became widely distributed.

Actually, tinware is made from tinplate—thin sheets of steel or iron dipped in molten tin. Tin by

Early tin cake pans *(below)* were often large by contemporary standards, indicative of the large families and appetites to match. The pan at the lower right is intricately designed permitting conversion to an angel cake (Turk Head) pan as it is shown here. It was patented as the "Centennial" in 1876.

itself being soft, malleable and having a low melting point, would not be practical for most household utensils.

The tinware objects above all directly pertain to brewing coffee and tea—early kettles, percolator and two canisters for storing tea.

The objects below are a syllabub mixer—a miniature up and down churn in tin, a kettle which fits into the top of the wood stove, and an 1878 patented percolator combining tin and copper. All objects shown on this page were made and assembled by hand except the handle on the 1878 percolator which was cast and inserted. Any similar object made in earthenware or cast iron would have been at least ten times the weight, so tinware was viewed as a "blessing" by the housewife whose tasks were many and neverending.

The Earthenware bottle, cullender, salt and butter bowl, along with similar pottery objects, were in everyday use along with iron and wooden utensils prior to the availability of tinware in America.

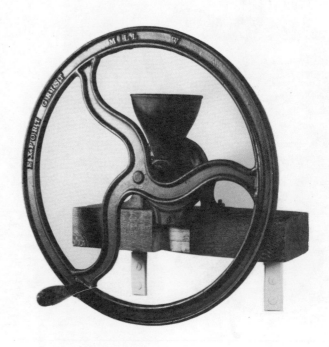

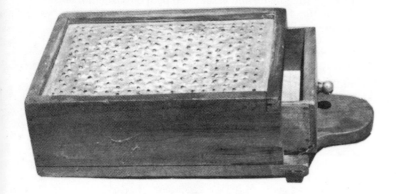

Some Early Kitchens

SHELVES in the kitchen of the *Patrick Henry Homestead* hold assorted earthenware and stoneware containers and tinware ladles and skimmers.

The small wall-mounted Export Grist Mill has a larger than usual power wheel for household grinders. Such devices were necessary to convert home-grown products into edible commodities.

The box-type grater has a handy removeable drawer and can be hung in the wall when not in use.

The table in James Monroe's *Ash Lawn* at Charlottesville, Virginia is laden with early artifacts including slipware, bowls, and candle molds. Note the shoulder harness which was quite a helpful device when one had to carry heavy wooden buckets full of water from well or spring house.

The artifacts around the fireplace and hearth at the *Mary Washington House* in Fredericksburg, Virginia, include trammels, wrought-iron toasters, skillets and wooden dough bowls, firkins and other objects—now rare but commonplace in early nineteenth century households.

The tin spice cabinet has eight drawers and could stand or be mounted on the kitchen wall.

The three hand-made pie crust rollers range in size from 5″ to 7½″ giving some perspective for the size of the early American hand-made spoons of horn.

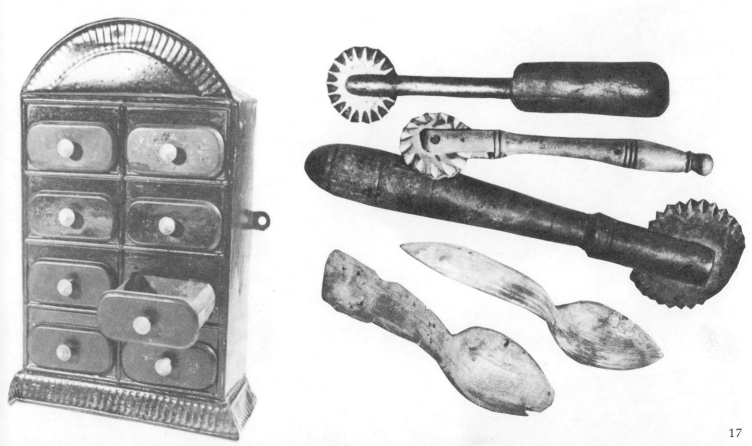

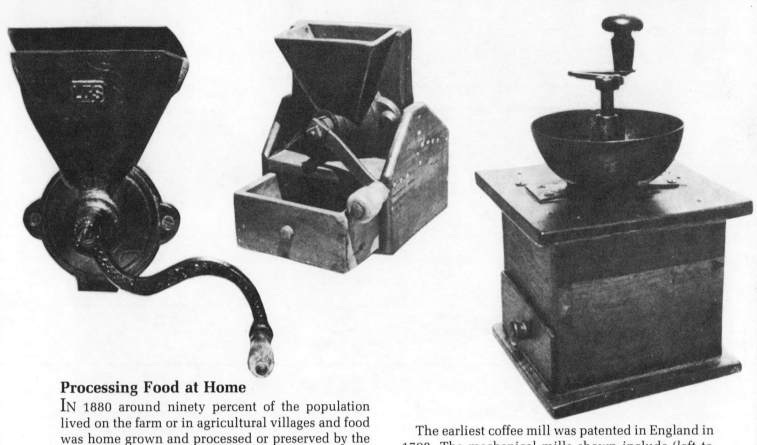

Processing Food at Home

IN 1880 around ninety percent of the population lived on the farm or in agricultural villages and food was home grown and processed or preserved by the family. Commodities purchased at the store were in bulk form; nutmeg, cloves and pepper were in natural form and had to be ground in a mill or scraped. Coffee came in green bean form and had to be ground and roasted.

The earliest coffee mill was patented in England in 1798. The mechanical mills shown include *(left to right)* root grinder, nutmeg grinder and traditional home coffee mill.

The tin coffee roaster *(lower left)* and wrought iron roaster *(lower right)* were both used at the open hearth and have a crank to move the ground coffee without opening the self-contained oven. The tin nutmeg grater lower left, was common to every household.

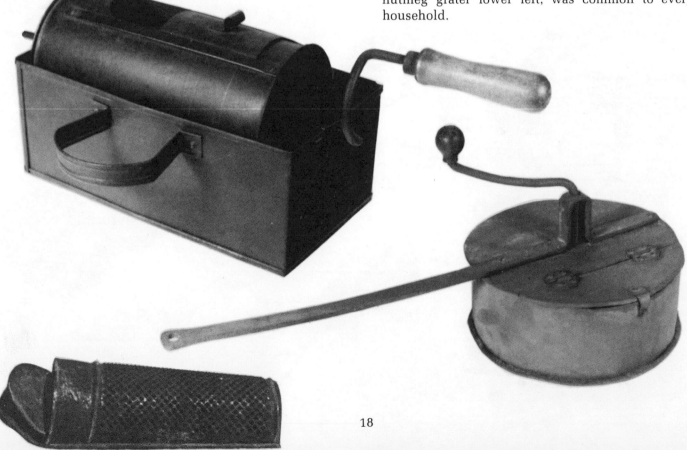

milk in pottery containers, and saw the milk and butter stored in the Spring house.

Milking and Churning

WHEN dawn broke on the early American homestead the livestock had already been tended and the dairy cows milked. Milking was menfolks' task, but the women had to get up almost as early to get the stove going for breakfast. Milk in the pail was basically a feminine concern—she did most of the churning the cream into butter, placing the butter-

The wooden dasher-churns were among the earliest used. The dasher had a round stick with a flat wooden cross nailed through the center of the lower end, with a wooden cover. After the cream is poured in the dasher is worked up and down until it froths, then swells, and breaks into curdly globules, finally gathering into a single mass. The so-called Bennington pottery churn was widely used in New England and these dasher-type devices were also made in Pennsylvania and Virginia. The rotary churn replaced all of these—it used less energy and made butter in a much shorter time.

The barrel churn (illustrated) is Spain's Improved #3, patented in 1872; others were made by Richmond Cedarworks, Richmond, Virginia

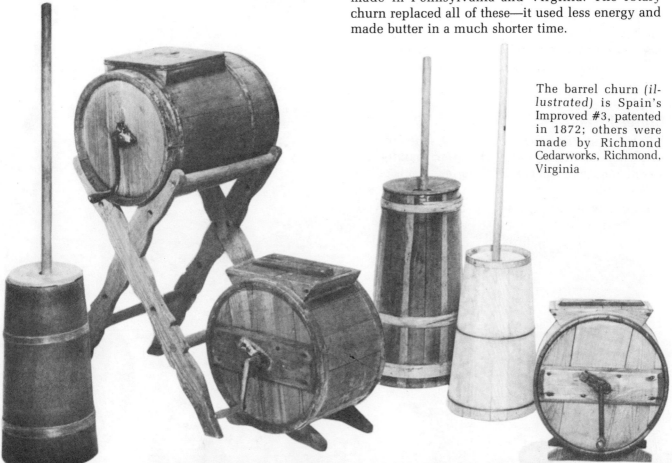

The pierced tin cheese molds *(left and below)* were often used, in conjunction with churning and butter making, to make egg cheese, similar to cottage cheese and a common dish among the Pennsylvania Dutch—often eaten along with apple butter.

When butter begins to gather, many makers replace the buttermilk with cold water and then work the butter with paddles in a tray—working in the salt and removing the excess buttermilk and water.

Some homemakers simply stored their butter in round wooden butter firkins or pottery crocks. Others were more fussy and used a wooden butter stamp or print with a carved design, creating a fancy-looking pat. The round wooden prints preceded the square pound prints and many were hand-carved at home, some with family initials.

In use, the prints and molds were soaked in boiling water, then in very cold water, to avoid the butter sticking. This process and the constant cleaning after use caused many early specimens to split or wear out.

Sent to market or used in exchange at the local general store, the decoration made it appear to be more carefully made and it served to identify the maker—so these objects were not always used just to be fancy.

Butter Prints

In contemporary times, with so few self-sufficient homesteads, the artifacts of butter making are among the Americana collectibles—remnants of our agrarian heritage.

Butter prints were made in a wide variety of

The case-type cylinder butter mold is typically a three-piece device consisting of a wooden container, handle and round plunger with the design carved in intaglio.

The case mold was patented April 17, 1866 and the date appears burned in the case on some specimens. This led to the popular belief that prints date only to that time but actually they were used at least a century earlier. Case molds exist in half-, one-, and two-pound sizes. Later versions were of glass and metal. These turn-of-the-century developments featured easier to cleaning.

designs. The most common types of wood were pine or poplar but some were made of apple, cherry, maple, walnut and oak.

Early prints were almost exclusively handmade, but after the mid-nineteenth century were by skilled artisans with specialized equipment (lathe routers, and mechanical tools), so early prints represent folk art and the later were craft. Later versions were often case molds sold at village country stores. Whether hand-carved or commercially made, the butter print was primarily a feminine household object, used, cleaned and cared for by the womenfolk.

Butchering

IN THE EARLY HOME the preparation of food was a constant process—not only in the daily preparation of meals from raw home grown grains and vegetables but in the preservation of fresh foods for future use. Fruit had to be picked, peeled, cooked and contained; animals had to be slaughtered, butchered and the meat processed, salted, smoked or cured.

Patent records indicate various mechanical devices for preparing both meat and vegetables; these devices worked on either the chopping or grinding principle. The earliest imitated the human hand motions in chopping—they had a moving beam motivated by a crank and gears which operated a chopping blade in up and down thrusts.

The early grinder involved a mangle made of iron spikes inserted in a wooden roller in a spiral row.

The crank turned the roller, shredding the inserted ingredients. The modern meat grinder emerged from this primitive device.

Although the first sausage cutters were patented in 1811 no meat stuffers were patented until 1824 but by 1850 there were several variant types of sausage stuffers manufactured in America.

Butchering was a regular fall chore. Some families invited neighbors to help and the event became a social frolic while completing a necessary task. Pork was the mainstay of the winter diet in most regions and at butchering time little of the hog was wasted.

On the morning of the butchering the family was up earlier than usual—each with specific duties. The big iron kettles were hung over the outdoor fireplace; a trough was set up and fires started; bucket after bucket of water was hand-pumped from the well and

A bench-type lard press and three more common type hand lard presses for squeezing lard from the skins and remainders of butchering.

The two round hand-sized objects are hog scrapers used to remove the bristles from the carcass after it was scalded.

The hand-made wooden press *(above)* was used to pack down ingredients in containers. The wrought iron nut cracker *(below)* was used for black walnuts. Many families spent long evening hours during the fall and winter months cracking and picking the meats from these difficult-to-shell delights, to be used in cakes and cookies and sold or traded at the general store for necessary cash or credit.

poured into the trough; butchering tools and equipment were made ready for the trip to the pig sty.

The hog was shot and the carcass hauled to the scalding trough where it was scraped clean of bristles and hung on a tall wooden tripod, hind feet up. The butchering followed, this being traditionally a masculine job, while the women finished the parts, cutting fat into cubes for rendering it into lard, grinding meat, boiling the juices and excess meat for use in pudding and scrapple, scraping entrails for stuffing sausage and cooking up the ingredients for making panhaus and scrapple. Even the feet were used—pickled.

Some families butchered as many as nine hogs at a time but three was a common number.

The early grinder *(upper right)* was hand-made of wood and wrought iron by a local blacksmith. The sturdy shaft and spiked iron grinder points created a coarse cutting, tearing the meat rather than sharply shearing it.

The two grinders below offer later models which were improvements in cast iron dating to the mid-century.

The wood and tin sausage stuffer was the earliest type known and this was the largest size measuring 19″ long compared to the typical 12″. These were replaced by the cast iron stuffers, much more convenient due to use of leverage. The one shown at the lower right is the large size measuring 28″ long, patented in 1858.

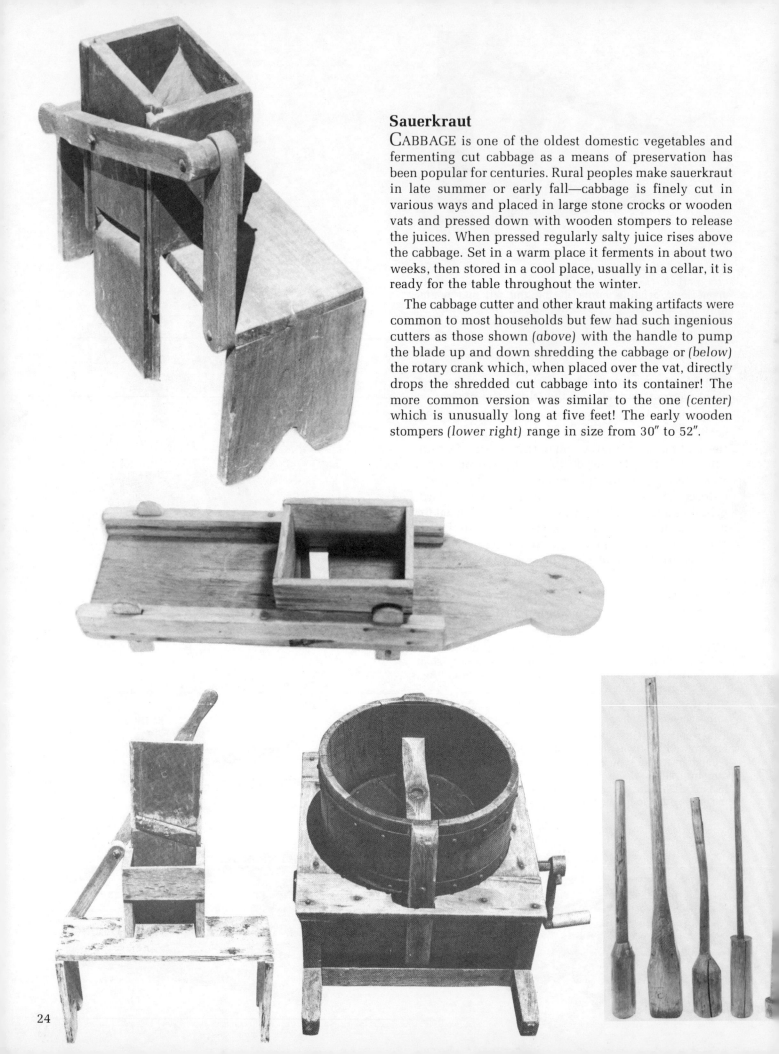

Sauerkraut

CABBAGE is one of the oldest domestic vegetables and fermenting cut cabbage as a means of preservation has been popular for centuries. Rural peoples make sauerkraut in late summer or early fall—cabbage is finely cut in various ways and placed in large stone crocks or wooden vats and pressed down with wooden stompers to release the juices. When pressed regularly salty juice rises above the cabbage. Set in a warm place it ferments in about two weeks, then stored in a cool place, usually in a cellar, it is ready for the table throughout the winter.

The cabbage cutter and other kraut making artifacts were common to most households but few had such ingenious cutters as those shown *(above)* with the handle to pump the blade up and down shredding the cabbage or *(below)* the rotary crank which, when placed over the vat, directly drops the shredded cut cabbage into its container! The more common version was similar to the one *(center)* which is unusually long at five feet! The early wooden stompers *(lower right)* range in size from 30″ to 52″.

Kitchen fireplace, John Marshall House (Chief Justice of the United States, 1801-1835) Richmond.

The wash stand was a characteristic piece in almost every bedroom, the wash bowl fitting into a cut-out portion of the top of the stand. The bowl and pitcher set consisted of ten pieces (with water lily decoration in this specimen) including chamber pot, soap and tooth brush holder, water pitcher and bowl and slop dispensers.

The dower chest is of poplar with its original hand-painted decoration. This typical Pennsylvania Dutch piece was actually made and decorated in the southern part of the Shenandoah Valley of Virginia (circa. 1800).

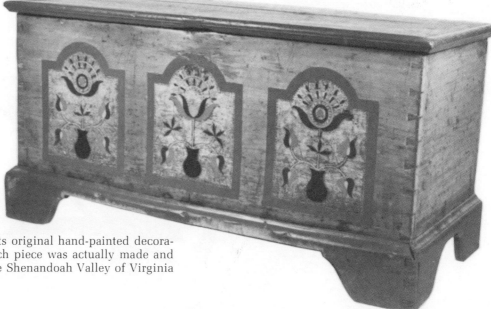

25

Cider and Apple Butter

CIDER was a national drink in early America—plenty of apples readily available and almost every neighborhood had a large mill or the farmstead had a mill of its own. Six to eight barrels of cider stored in the root cellar wouldn't be unusual. Obviously there was plenty of cider and distilled apple brandy too!

Sweet cider starting to ferment was boiled in brass kettles to a syrupy thickness. This was used as tart molasses, a base for mince meat and even as a sauce poured over pancakes.

When cider fermented and became "hard" it was a real intoxicant—a major concern of the Temperance enthusiasts. But hard cider *was* distilled into apple brandy and many a farmer took a nip on a winter morning before his outdoor chores.

Almost every farm had apple trees and the equipment to make the most of the fruit. Pruning and grafting were masculine tasks, but processing was primarily the work of the women. All played a role in the harvest and the activities that followed—cider pressing, snitzing (cutting up) and apple butter boiling frolics were common.

Snitzing is the peeling, coring and cutting of apples into sections. Some snitzing ended with the slices exposed to the sun for drying, to be used throughout the year as dried fruit for pies.

Such activities were often held the evening prior to a boiling, allowing an early start as a boiling takes considerable time. Boiling starts with a 30 or 40 gallon copper kettle placed over an outdoor fire in which cider and apple snitz are cooked along with spices and continually stirred. This is a time-consuming task involving continual fire tending and turning the long goose-neck stirrer or paddle. The finished product was poured into crocks.

Apple Mill
The apple chopper and press shown is the 1865 "Latest Improved Buckeye Junior" by P. R. Mast & Co., Springfield, O. Original patent issued in 1846. Each new version had more iron. This device cuts the apples into small pieces, and presses out the juice by the front-screw device.

This tasty spread was commonly on the table at all meals to be used on bread, biscuits and even mixed in with cottage cheese.

Artifacts of the apple-boiling tradition include copper kettles and holding rings of iron, stirrers, apple butter storage crocks, and apple peelers.

Apple parer

One of the first American domestic machines was the apple parer. In 1803 the first patent was issued to Moses Coates of Chester Co., Penna. Typical of hundreds of later types it featured a rotating fork to impale the apple and a special blade held against it to pare it. Early specimens are of wood with metal fork and blade turned by a crank.

Mid-century peelers made of cast iron became increasingly complex. Some turned the apple and moved the blade around it by use of a series of rotating gears.

Sugaring, Syrup, Honey

BY EARLY MARCH farmers in many parts of the country started preparing for sugaring. They checked the sap buckets to make certain they were tight and hoops secure, spouts were checked and tubs and kettles washed and loaded on the sledge.

When the season arrives when it freezes at night and thaws during the day (bright sunny day with cold west winds) there should be a good run of sap from the maples. This is usually in March but may extend until the frost is out of the ground and the buds swell. A small camp might "set" from two to three hundred sap buckets and get between 25 and 40 gallons of syrup. But it takes as much as fifty gallons of sap to boil down to a gallon of syrup—a great deal of carrying filled buckets and hours of

The beesmoker (below) was used to assist in retrieving honey; the round object is a "bee liner" and the jars were early style honey jars. Bee liners were home-made devices which were used to place rambling bees which were released only to be followed to their hive.

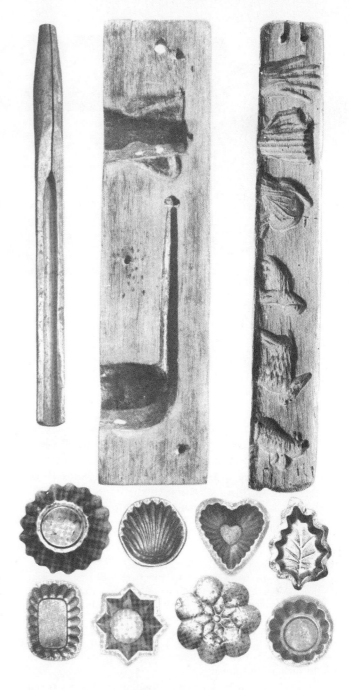

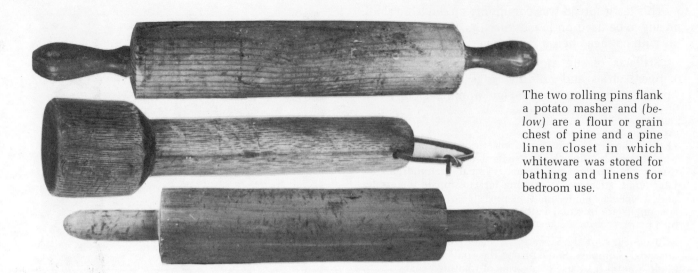

The two rolling pins flank a potato masher and *(below)* are a flour or grain chest of pine and a pine linen closet in which whiteware was stored for bathing and linens for bedroom use.

tending fire to boil from 1,200 to 2,000 gallons of sap.

When white sugar became common, maple sugar was special, not just "tree lasses" as it was referred to earlier, and more and more was made into cake sugar.

Vermont is best known for maple sugar but it is also produced in Canada, New Hampshire, New York, Ohio, Pennsylvania, Wisconsin, West Virginia and western Virginia. Once the main source of sweetening in these sections, the artifacts associated with this harvest are part of the self-sufficiency of our rural past.

Honey

No honey bees were found by the first white settlers at Plymouth Rock, so they imported them from the Old World. Early settlers made skeps so bees would use them instead of hiving in hollow trees where their product—honey and wax—was so hard to find and retrieve. The skeps (a hive made of tightly braided straw) were often placed in a loft or covered wood-shed to protect the bees in the bitter cold winter months.

In areas where maple sap was not available, honey was the only source of sweetners and the wax made fine candles.

Flies

Insects were a major problem, and housewives have battled them from the beginning. Flies, fleas, mosquitoes and similar insects have been responsible for much illness and for the pollution of food. Nevertheless, man did little to control them, and it wasn't until the 1860's that wire mesh screens were invented for windows and doors—so various types of fly swatters and fly paper were household tools to combat such annoying pests.

Keeping Warm

STOVES were made by many iron furnaces and forges for heating, cooking, laundry and butchering tasks. The Franklin type stove shown *(upper left)* is a late model as is the wood burning parlor stove.

After Benjamin Franklin invented the cast iron plate stove almost every home sought such devices because the fireplace consumed an astounding quantity of fuel in proportion to the heat provided. The cast iron stoves concentrated heat and conserved fuel—also reduced the labor involved in cutting, hauling and refueling.

The intricate perculator contained the coffee and liquid when in use; but was complex in assembly as shown. Made of brass with tin inner fittings; it seems like a considerable effort involved when compared with making a simple cup of instant!

Containers

WHEN the family went to the general store the purchases were usually unprocessed and unpackaged. They bought yards of material rather than clothing; cheese came in large wheels and was cut to order—approximately! Each sale was measured, weighed and placed in the family shopping basket—paper bags were not developed until the late 1850's and there was little pre-packaging except in wholesale lots such as 120 pounds of coffee or a 199 lb barrel of flour. Tea, sugar, beans, crackers, rice, grains were sold from open counter containers. Vinegar, kerosene, molasses and other liquids were sold in bulk directly from large vats or barrels. Obviously the household required assorted containers for these necessities to hold until needed for baking, preserving or consumption.

The device (upper left) was used in gathering huckleberries; illustrated are baskets for gathering eggs, marketing, for washing—common to every home; barrels for sugar, flour, molasses, cider and vinegar and pumps to remove liquids were in all basements.

Tin utilitarian ware gradually replaced almost all the heavy stoneware and iron utensils. Those shown include the large flour cannister and the commode set which has the original stencil decorations.

Mud and Boots

CONTEMPORARY AMERICANS have little contact with mud—early settlers despised it! Man could move around on ice and snow by use of sledges and sleighs but when the thaw came there was little transportation in mud, so it often meant waiting for wind and sun to dry it up.

Footwear was constantly caked with layers of mud so boot scrapers were common at most homne entrances and bookjacks were readily available to aid in taking off their dirty boots or shoes. Illustrated are a wrought iron scraper and simple pinewood boot jack. The child's size boot-jack bench is a rare piece.

Interior photograph features pine Welsh cupboard with pottery utensils including sgraffito and slipware of Pennsylvania origin and various early kitchen utensils.

Acknowledgements

THE author and illustrator wish to express sincere appreciation to the Association for the Preservation of Virginia Antiquities for assistance and cooperation.

Credit is noted throughout for the permission to photograph specific sites including the John Marshall House, Richmond, Virginia; Mary Washington House, Fredericksburg; Ash Lawn (Highlands, home of President James Monroe) Charlottesville, Sublets Tavern, Powhatan, Scotchtown (Home of Patrick Henry) Hanover County, Virginia.

We are also grateful to the following individuals for their kind and generous assistance; Mrs. Mary Dee Boswell, Cooperstown, N.Y.; Mr. and Mrs. Terry Smith, Brandermill, Virginia; Bill and Helen Holt, owners of the Curiosity Shop, Elkton, Virginia; Mrs. Carolyn Holmes, Charlottesville; Mrs. Viola Fleming and Kenneth Ferguson, Richmond; Mrs. Edward Fulwider, Scotchtown; Mr. and Mrs. Tom Layman, Powhatan and Mrs. Levin Huston III and Mrs. Donald J. Kenneweg, Fredericksburg, Virginia.

(Rear Cover) Cast iron baking pan and tin cookie-candy molds (upper).

1842 Alphabet sampler, pine cutting boards, one shaped as a fish; grits (corn) sieve (right).

(Lower left) Rubbing board used in washing. (Right) Dippers and a well-carved Springerlie board for Christmas cookies.